Hedgehogs

Julie Murray

Abdo
NOCTURNAL ANIMALS
Kids

abdopublishing.com

Published by Abdo Kids, a division of ABDO, PO Box 398166, Minneapolis, Minnesota 55439.

Printed in the United States of America, North Mankato, Minnesota.

102017

012018

THIS BOOK CONTAINS RECYCLED MATERIALS

Photo Credits: iStock, Minden Pictures, Shutterstock

Production Contributors: Teddy Borth, Jennie Forsberg, Grace Hansen

Design Contributors: Christina Doffing, Candice Keimig, Dorothy Toth

Publisher's Cataloging-in-Publication Data

Names: Murray, Julie, author.

Title: Hedgehogs / by Julie Murray.

Description: Minneapolis, Minnesota : Abdo Kids, 2018. | Series: Nocturnal animals | Includes glossary, index and online resource (page 24).

Identifiers: LCCN 2017908179 | ISBN 9781532104060 (lib.bdg.) | ISBN 9781532105180 (ebook) | ISBN 9781532105746 (Read-to-me ebook)

Subjects: LCSH: Hedgehogs--Juvenile literature. | Nocturnal animals--Juvenile literature.

Classification: DDC 599.33--dc23

LC record available at https://lccn.loc.gov/2017908179

Table of Contents

Hedgehogs

It is dark. Something is **grunting**. What is it?

A hedgehog!

Hedgehogs live in many places.

They live in forests and fields.

Some live in deserts.

They are small animals. Most weigh about 1.5 pounds (0.7 kg).

They have long noses.

Their eyes are small.

They have sharp **quills**. **Fur** is on their faces and bellies.

They sleep in nests during the day. They eat at night.

They eat insects. They like worms and eggs too.

They live for two to seven years.

Features of Hedgehogs

fur

long nose

quills

small eyes

Glossary

grunt
a noise, like a pig's snort, that hedgehogs sometimes make when eating.

fur
the short, fine, soft hair of some animals.

quills
the hallow, sharp spines of a hedgehog.

Index